中华五福

Designs of Chinese Blessings

Good Fortune

主　编／黄全信

副主编／黄迎　李进

编　委／吴曼丽　赵义　张玉玲　李小伟　周利

王博　齐学文　韩菁

翻　译／周晔

华语教学出版社
SINOLINGUA

First Edition 2003

ISBN 7-80052-889-8

Copyright 2003 by Sinolingua

Published by Sinolingua

24 Baiwanzhuang Road, Beijing 100037, China

Tel: (86) 10-68995871/68326333

Fax: (86) 10-68326333

E-mail: hyjx @263.net

Printed by Beijing Foreign Languages Printing House

Distributed by China International

Book Trading Corporation

35 Chegongzhuang Xilu, P.O.Box 399

Beijing 100044, China

Printed in the People's Republic of China

目 录
contents

人臻五福　花满三春

吉祥一词，始见于《易经》："吉事有祥。"《左传》有："是何祥也？吉祥焉在？"《庄子》则有："虚室生白，吉祥止止。"《注疏》云："吉者，福善之事；祥者，嘉庆之征。"

吉祥二字，在甲骨文中被写作"吉羊"。上古人过着游牧生活，羊肥大成群是很"吉祥"的事，在古器物的铭文中多有"吉羊"。《说文》云："羊，祥也。"

吉祥，是美好、幸运的形象；吉祥，是人类最迷人的主题。艺术，最终都是把理想形象化；吉祥图，是中华吉祥文化最璀璨的明珠。旧时有联："善果皆欢喜，香云普吉祥。"吉祥图有：吉祥如意、五福吉祥等。

五福，是吉祥的具体。福、禄、寿、喜、财，在民间被称为五福；福星、禄星、寿星、喜神、财神，在仙界被尊为五福神。五福最早见于《尚书》："五福：一曰寿，二曰富，三曰

康宁，四曰攸好德，五曰考终命。"旧时有联："三阳临吉地，五福萃华门。"吉祥图有：五福捧寿、三多五福等。

福，意为幸福美满。《老子》："福兮，祸所伏。"《韩非子》："全富贵之谓福。"旧时有联："香焚一炷，福赐三多。"吉祥图有：福在眼前、纳福迎祥、翘盼福音、天官赐福等。

禄，意为高官厚禄。《左传》："介之推不言禄，禄亦弗及。"《汉书》："身宠而载高位，家温而食厚禄。"旧时有联："同科十进士，庆榜三名元。"吉祥图有：禄位高升、福禄寿禧、天赐禄爵、加官进禄等。

寿，意为健康长寿。《庄子》："人，上寿百岁，中寿八十，下寿六十。"《诗经》："如南山之寿，不骞不崩。"旧时有联："同臻寿域，共跻春台。"吉祥图有：寿星高照、鹤寿千年、富贵寿考、蟠桃献寿等。

喜，意为欢乐喜庆。《国语》："固庆其喜而吊其忧。"韦昭注："喜犹福也。"旧时有联："笑到几时方合口，坐来无日不开怀。"吉祥图有：喜上眉梢、双喜临门、端阳喜庆、皆大欢喜等。

财，意为发财富有。《荀子》："务本节用财无极。"旧时有联："生意兴隆通四海，财源茂盛达三江。"吉祥图有：财源滚滚、招财进宝、喜交财运、升官发财等。

吉祥图，不仅有"五福"之内涵，而且是

绘画艺术和语言艺术的珠联璧合。在绘画上，体现了中国画主要的表现手段——线的魅力，给人以美感，令人赏心悦目。吉祥图虽多出自民间画工之手，却多有顾恺之"春蚕吐丝"之韵，曹仲达"曹衣出水"之美，吴道子"吴带当风"之妙；在语言上，通俗和普及了古代文化，吉祥图多配有一句浓缩成四个字的吉语祥词，给人以吉祥，令人心驰神往。

《中华五福吉祥图典》，汇集了我数代家传和几十年收藏的精品吉祥图，可谓美不胜收。其中既有明之典雅，又有清之华丽；既有皇家之富贵，又有民间之纯朴；既有北方之粗犷，又有南方之秀美……按五福全书分成福、禄、寿、喜、财五集，每集吉祥图 119 幅，共 595 幅。除同类图案外，均按笔画顺序编排。基本包括了中国传统吉祥图的各个方面，并对每幅图作了考证和诠释，使之图文并茂，相得益彰。

五福人人喜，吉祥家家乐。吉祥图是中国的，也是世界的，故以汉英对照出版。《中华五福吉祥图典》会给您带来吉祥，给您全家带来幸福。

黄全信于佩实斋
2003 年 1 月 1 日

◎中华五福吉祥图典

福

福 禄 寿 喜 财

May People Enjoy a Life Full of Blessings, and Let Flowers Bloom Throughout Spring Time

The word jixiang (meaning lucky, propitious, or auspicious) is mentioned in Chinese ancient books and writings as early as in the Zhou Dynasty.

The word jixiang was written as jiyang (lucky sheep) on oracle bones. To the ancient Chinese, who led a nomadic life, large herds of well-fed sheep were auspicious things, and the word jiyang also appeared in engravings on ancient utensils.

To have good luck is mankind's eternal desire. While art records man's ideals, good luck pictures are the most brilliant part of the Chinese good luck culture. An old couplet says that kindness leads to happiness and good luck. Typical good luck pictures are: good luck and heart's content, good luck with five blessings, etc.

The five blessings – good fortune, high salary and a good career, longevity, happiness, and wealth – are the concrete forms of good luck , and there are five kinds of gods presiding over these blessings. The five blessings as they are first mentioned in Chinese literature are not quite the same as the five which are talked about today, though they are quite similar. An old couplet says that as the land of good luck bathes in the Sun, a prosperous family is granted all the blessings. Typical good luck pictures are: long-term enjoyment of all five blessings, more blessings, etc.

Good fortune means happiness and complete satisfaction. Ancient Chinese philosophers, including Lao Zi, all commented on the notion of good fortune. An old couplet says to burn incense to beg for more blessings. Good luck pictures in this theme include good fortune for today, blessings from above, etc.

High salary means handsome salaries at prestigious posts. In old times, Chinese attached great significance to academic excellence, which led in turn to high positions in government. An old couplet says may you distinguish yourselves in the royal examinations and rank at the top of the list. Good luck pictures in this theme used in this book include big improvements in salary and post, salary and position bestowed from heaven, etc.

Longevity refers to good health and a long life. As Zhuangzhou said, and the *Book of Songs* records, longevity is the universal wish of mankind. As wished in an old couplet, to grow to a long life together is a joyful experience . This book has the following good luck pic -

中华五福吉祥图典

福

福禄寿喜财

tures concerning longevity: high above shines the star of longevity, live to be 1, 000 years with white hair, and offer the flat peach to wish for longevity, etc.

Happiness refers to happy events and celebrations. Happy events should be celebrated, while those with worries should be consoled according to ancient Chinese literature. An old Chinese couplet says, why not keep on laughing as all days are filled with happiness. Good luck pictures on this theme included in this book include double happiness visits at the door, all's well that ends well, etc.

Wealth means getting rich and having plentiful things. Ancient Chinese believed that the secret to endless wealth is to be down-to-earth and prudent. Illustrating the concept of wealth is an old couplet: a prosperous business deals with people from all corners of the world, and wealth rolls in from afar. Typical good luck pictures of this type include in comes wealth, get rich and win high positions, etc.

Good luck pictures not only incorporate the five blessings but the art of painting and language as well. The beautiful lines of these pictures, done in the style of traditional Chinese painting, provide the viewers with artistic enjoyment which is pleasing to the eyes and heart. Though mostly the work of folk artists, they exhibit a level of craftsmanship worthy of the great and famous masters. The language adopted in these pictures

serves to popularize ancient culture, and the four-char-
acter good luck phrase accompanying almost every picture depicts an attractive scene. *Designs of Chinese
Blessings* is a compilation of special good luck pictures
passed down in my family for several generations as
well those which I have been collecting for dozens of
years. Their beauty is beyond description. They com-
bine the elegance of the Ming Dynasty and the magnifi-
cence of the Qing Dynasty, the nobility of the royal
family and the modesty of the common people, the
boldness of the north and the delicacy of the south.
The book consists of five sections: good fortune, high
salary and a good career, longevity, happiness, and
wealth. With 119 pictures in each section, the whole
book contains 595 pictures and is a complete represent-
ation of the various aspects of traditional Chinese good
luck pictures. On top of this, research has been done
on each picture, and the interpretations complement
the visuals nicely.

As the five blessings are the aspiration of each in-
dividual, good luck delights all households. The good
luck pictures originated in China and their good message should benefit all people of this world. May the
Designs of Chinese Blessings bring good luck to your life
and happiness to your family.

Huang Quanxin
Jan.1, 2003

一方平安

Peace in this place

《礼记》："共工氏之霸九州也，其子曰后士，能平九州，故祀以为社。"土地崇拜始于氏族社会，社神是与天神相应的大神。《通俗编》："今日社神，俱呼土地。"土地则是小神，管一段地面，保一方平安，旧俗祭土地神以求丰稔。

The worship of land started in the clan society. The god of land is the matching big god of the heavenly god. The god of land is a small god, only in charge of one patch of land, and protects this area's safety. It was also an old tradition to sacrifice to the land for gains in the harvest.

福
Good Fortune

一家之主

The master of the family

灶君是旧时民间信仰的灶神，供
奉于灶头，被认为能掌管一家祸福。
旧俗腊月二十三或二十四日为"送灶
日"，以纸马饴糖等送灶神上天。因
灶神有"上天言事"之特权，故民间
往往在灶头贴上"上天言好事，下界
降吉祥"的对联。除夕又迎回，称为
"迎灶日"。

According to folk wisdom, Zao Jun is the
kitchen god who resides in the hood of the kitchen
and should be worshipped. It is said that he is in
charge of the fate of the family. The 22nd and
23rd of December in the lunar calendar are the
"Farewell to the Kitchen God" days. People burn
paper money and paper horses to see the kitchen
god off to heaven. People also put a nice couplet
on the kitchen hood. At the end of the lunar year,
people will welcome the kitchen god back. This is
called "Welcome the Kitchen God Back" day.

一家之主

The master of the family

古代宫廷及官宦人家多用黄羊祭灶，后百姓也如此。祭灶时，在灶王像面前摆上供品，除瓜果梨桃，最主要的是供黄羊。把一只黄羊平放在木槽中，放在供桌后面，称之为"黄羊祭灶"。祭后"送王上天"，大家再分食供品。

In ancient times, royal families and noble families offered Mongolian gazelles as tribute to the kitchen god. Later, ordinary people followed suit. When they conducted the sacrifice ceremony, the Mongolia gazelle was the most important sacrifice, besides the fruits. The gazelle would be placed in the middle of a wood notch. After the ceremony, people would divide the food among themselves.

◎中华五福吉祥图典

福

福禄寿喜财

一家之主

The master of the family

传说古代有一叫阴子方的人，在腊月二十三做饭时，灶神突现，于是阴子方立刻跪下叩头拜神。跟着他把家中养的唯一一只黄羊杀了，奉祀灶神。从此以后阴子方家财运大发，后世人多效仿。灶王为一家之主，带来福水善火。

It was said that a man named Yin Zifang immediately got down on his knees and made kowtows to the kitchen god when the god suddenly showed up while he was cooking on the 23rd of December in the Chinese lunar calendar. Then he killed the only Mongolian gazelle that he had at home as a sacrifice to the god. After that, his family made a great fortune. People of later generations often followed his lead. The kitchen god is believed to be the master of the family, and will bring lucky water and blessed fire to the family.

中华五福吉祥图典

福

福禄寿喜财

一路平安

Safe journey

衣、食、住、行，是人类生活的四大需求。古代交通不便，出门行路艰难。上路时燃放爆竹，祭祀路神以求一路平安。路神，传说是上古神话人物共工之子修，修喜远游终死路途。到了两千多年后的汉朝，修被人们尊为路神。

Food, clothing, housing and transportation are the four basic needs of human life. In ancient times it was not convenient for people to travel. People normally set off firecrackers before they left home to gain the blessing of the road god. The god of the road is called Xiu, son of the legendary Gong Gong, who loved travel and died during the course of his journeys. Two thousand years later, Xiu was respectfully considered to be the god of the road in the Han Dynasty.

◎中华五福吉祥图典

福

福 禄 寿 喜 财

二龙戏珠

Two dragons play ball

Designs of Chinese Blessings

二龙戏珠源于民间的耍龙灯，有庆丰年、祈吉祥之意。龙，是华夏先祖的图腾，后来一直是最大的吉祥物。"飞龙在天，犹圣人之在王位"。历代帝王多自诩为真龙天子。龙在中国被尊为至高无上的神，炎黄子孙自称是龙的传人。

This saying originated from a folk play which celebrated the harvest year and asked for blessings from heaven. The dragon is the totem of China's ancestors and has always been the most important auspicious animal in Chinese folklore. All the emperors in Chinese history have thought of themselves as dragon princes. The dragon is also respected as the supreme god of China, and it is said that all Chinese are the offsprings of dragons.

福

福禄寿喜财

十二章

Twelve patterns

十二章是古代皇帝在隆重场合所穿礼服的装饰纹样，均有取意：日、月、星辰，取其照临；山，取其稳重；龙，取其应变；华步，取其文丽；宗彝，取其忠孝；藻，取其洁净；火，取其光明；粉末，取其滋养；黼，取其决断；黻，取其明辨。

These are the badges and decorations on the ceremonial costumes of ancient emperors, each with a different meaning. The sun, moon and stars are used to mean shining light; the mountain to mean stability; the dragon to mean flexibility; fire for its lighting power; and powder for its nourishment; etc..

人文初祖

The ancestor of civilization

黄帝，是中华民族的始祖。传说在位百年，教民养蚕、制衣、建宫室、造舟车，发明了算数、音律，制定了天文历法，还命仓颉创造了文字，开创了中华民族灿烂的文化。远古文明绝非一人所为，但旧时有"功归圣人"之说。

The Yellow Emperor is the ancestor of all Chinese. It is said that he taught people how to raise silkworms, make clothing, build ships and he also invented methods of calculation, musical styles, and ordered Cang Jie to create Chinese characters. He was also said to have laid the rules for the astronomical almanac. He started glorious Chinese culture. It is obviously not a single man's effort to establish an ancient civilization. But normally the sage is credited with all these achievements.

◎中华五福吉祥图典

福

福 禄 寿 喜 财

八吉祥

Eight auspicious things

　　八吉祥，亦称八宝：法螺、法
轮、宝伞、白盖、莲花、宝瓶、金
鱼、盘长，均是佛家的法物。第一件
法螺妙音吉祥，所以统称"八吉祥"。
俗称第八件盘长为八吉，又以盘长代
表八宝。八宝常作为祈祷吉祥幸福的
象征之物。

There are eight auspicious things in Buddhism: the triton, the Wheel of the Law, the can-
opy, the divine shield, the lotus, the bottle, the
goldfish, and the knitting knot. The sound of the
triton is considered to be the sound of luck. The
eighth item – the knitting knot – is often used to
represent the eight things. All together, these
eight things are called the eight lucks. They are
often considered to be the symbol of blessings for
fortune and happiness.

◎中华五福吉祥图典

福

福禄寿喜财

Good Fortune

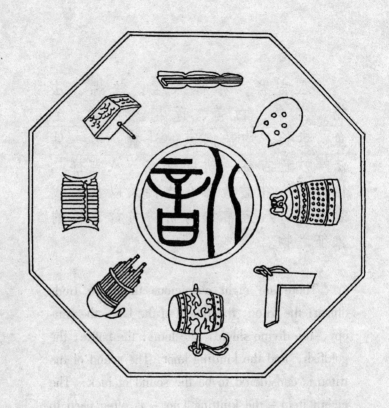

八音图

The picture of eight
musical instruments

八音，是中国古代对乐器的统
称。指金、石、土、革、丝、木、
匏、竹八类。钟、铃等属金类，磬等
属石类，埙等属土类，鼓等属革类，
琴、瑟等属丝类，柷敔等属木类，
笙、竽等属匏类，管、籥等属竹类。
众乐妙音，吉祥喜庆。

This is a summary of Chinese ancient musical
instruments. They belong to eight categories,
namely, gold, stone, earth, leather, string,
wood, bamboo, and gourd. When all the different kinds of music are played together, it is considered to be a very propitious occasion.

◎中华五福吉祥图典

福

福禄寿喜财

福
Good Fortune

八 音 图

The picture of eight
musical instruments

钟、磬、琴、箫、笙、埙、鼓
柷、围八种乐器为八音。美妙的音
乐，可以给人带来愉悦，也可给人带
来吉祥。孔子讲坛环植以杏并伴以琴
瑟，使学子赏心悦目，故杏坛、弦歌
也成了学校的美称。孔子曰："兴于
诗，立于礼，成于乐。"

Here are eight musical instruments. It is said
that the beautiful music can bring pleasure to people as well as fortune. Confucius once planted
apricot trees around his lecturing platform, and
the apricot trees and the music made students feel
enchanted. Because of this his school is called the
"apricot arena". The "string song" also became
the metaphor of his school.

◎中华五福吉祥图典

福

福 禄 寿 喜 财

Good Fortune

八仙过海

*Eight immortals cross
the ocean*

明《东游记传》：八仙共赴蟠桃大会，归途遇海。吕洞滨曰不得乘云，于是李铁拐、汉钟离、张果老、何仙姑、蓝采和、吕洞宾、韩湘子、曹国舅，分别以拐杖、鼓、纸驴、竹罩、拍板、箫管、花篮、玉笏为工具，乘之渡海。后世说："八仙过海，各显其能。"

Legend has it that eight immortals went together to the peach feast held in heaven. On their way back, they came to a big ocean. Lü Dong-bing, who was one of the immortals, said that they should not ride on clouds. The other seven immortals respectively used a stick, a drum, a paper donkey, a bamboo shade, a clip, a tube, and a flower basket as riding tools to cross the ocean. Later people said, eight immortals cross the ocean, each shows his/her own capabilities.

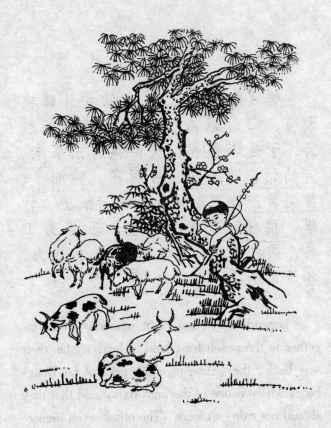

九阳启泰

Nine suns shine

　　《楚辞·远游》："朝濯发于汤谷兮，夕晞余身兮九阳。"九为多，阳即日。图以"九羊"谐音"九阳"，"羊"又为古"祥"字。启泰即开泰之意。寓走运，好兆头。"九阳启泰"意为吉日高悬、祥光普照，预兆好运、万事如意。

　　In Chinese folklore nine means a large quantity. "Nine sheep" sounds like "nine suns" when pronounced in Chinese. Sheep also sounds like "luck" in Chinese. This saying means the sign of good luck with the lucky sun shining above.

中华五福吉祥图典

福

福禄寿喜财

九九消寒图

Winter picture

在中国的节气中，"冬至"过后，便进入了"数九"。经过九九八十一天才能迎来明媚的春天。旧时有"九九歌"，还有"九九消寒图"。九九消寒图多以优美的日历形式出现，品种很多，如：梅花消寒图、葫芦消寒图、文字消寒图等。

In Chinese solar terms, after the Winter Solstice there are still 81 days in the season of winter. Only after that comes the bright spring. In old times, winter pictures always appeared on various beautiful calendars.

◎中华五福吉祥图典

福

福禄寿喜财

三圣同辉

Three sages' glory

孔子、老子、释迦牟尼，是对中国影响最大的儒教、道教、佛教的创始人。二千五百年前左右，人类的发展进入了一个崭新的阶段，产生了一些超越时空的先哲，如老子、孔子、释迦牟尼、苏格拉底等。

Confucius, Laozi and Sakyamuni were respectively the founders of Confucianism, Taoism and Buddhism. About 2,500 years ago, the development of mankind moved to a brand new stage, together with the appearance of sages like Laozi, Confucius, Sakyamuni, etc.

三合九重

*The summary of auspicious
things in a picture*

日月三合九重八卦十二分图，为明末画家萧云从所绘。图中包括：状如法轮的太极图、绘有三足乌的太阳、绘有玉兔的太阴，以及八卦图、九宫图、十二生肖图、二十八星座图等。是集先秦吉祥图之大成，带有神秘的色彩。

Xiao Yuncong of the late Ming Dynasty painted this picture. Many different things are included in the picture, such as the *Taiji* picture with the shape of the Buddhist wheel, the sun with a three-foot-turtle, the moon with a jade rabbit, Eight Trigrams, 12 symbolic animals, 28 constellations, etc. This has been considered a masterpiece before the Qin Dynasty, noted as a work of great mystery.

中华五福吉祥图典

福

福禄寿喜财

三阳开泰

Three suns shine

图以"三羊"谐音"三阳"。三阳为乾卦卦象，示阳盛阴衰。开泰为卦名，示乾上坤下，天地相交而万物开通。三阳开泰，语出《易卦》。正月为泰卦，三阳生于下，取其冬去春来，阴消阳长，有吉享之象，多用于岁首祝颂吉祥。

This picture uses three sheep to stand for three suns, as sheep and sun sound the same in Chinese, and it means the interchange of Yin and Yang. This originated in *The Book of Changes*, and means that nature changes according to scientific terms. This saying is often used as a eulogy at the beginning of the New Year.

◎中华五福吉祥图典

福

福 禄 寿 喜 财

三阳开泰

Three suns shine

羊，温顺又合群，所以过着游牧生活的上古先人，以羊肥大成群为最吉祥的事，故"吉祥"最早写为"吉羊"。三阳开泰是指冬去春来，万象更新，旧时多用作春节时的祝颂语，并有画三只羊的吉祥图，"羊"与"阳"谐音。

Sheep are genteel and team-oriented. Therefore, the nomadic Chinese ancestors considered big flocks of sheep as the most fortunate sign. This saying implies the seasonal change of winter and spring.

福

福禄寿喜财

三纲五常

Ethical standards

"三纲五常"是中国封建社会的
"礼"，也泛指旧礼教和伦理道德，是
汉董仲舒根据孔子的学说提出的。
"三纲"即"君为臣纲，父为子纲，
夫为妻纲。" "五常"即"仁、义、
礼、智、信。"图中的三"缸"酒，
五人"尝"，乃谐音取意。

These are the ethics of Chinese feudal society, which generally refers to all old ethical and
moral standards, mentioned by Dong Zhongshu of
the Han Dynasty, according to Confucian sayings.
The Three Principles are: the subject should obey
the monarch; sons should obey their fathers;
wives should obey their husbands. The Five Man-
ners are morality, duty, rites, wisdom, and faith-
fulness. The principles of the ethics are represent-
ed as three jars of wine and five people try their
taste in the picture, as "principle" sounds the
same as "jar" and "manner" as "taste" in Chinese.

福

福 禄 寿 喜 财

人皇氏

天皇氏

地皇氏

三皇开世

*Three emperors founded
the world*

三皇是传说中的远古帝王，最早见于《吕氏春秋》。三皇有多种说法，《史记·补三皇本纪》载：天地初立，有天皇、地皇、人皇。传说天皇十三头，地皇十一头，人皇九头，皆龙身。到了人皇时期，人类才告别了动物世界。

These are the three legendary emperors, first recorded in the *Lü's Annals*. These three emperors are respectively the emperors of heaven, earth and mankind. It is said that only when the era of the human emperor began did human beings start to leave the animal world.

中华五福吉祥图典

福

福 禄 寿 喜 财

大　吉

Big luck

大　吉

Big luck

《礼记·郊特性》："陶匏（葫芦）以象天地性。"《诗经·大雅续篇》："绵绵瓜瓞，民之初生。"葫芦是龙女娲与虎伏羲的共同身，是阴阳合体。早在新石器时代的仰韶文化中，葫芦就已经成为孕育生命的神物。葫芦又"多子"，取意吉祥。

The gourd is androgynous, it is used here to symbolize the combination of the male and the female. Traced back to the Yang Shao culture in the New Stone Age, the gourd had already become a divine symbol of nourishing new life, because the gourd contains so many seeds.

Good Fortune

大 福 寿

Big fortune and longevity

《尚书·洪范》:"五福:一曰寿，二曰富，三曰康宁，四曰攸好德，五曰考终命。"旧时春联常有五福，如"三阳临春地，五福萃华门。"福是一切吉祥的概括。图中的佛手、寿桃、桔子、荔枝为吉祥物，音寓福寿吉利。

In the *Book of Historical Document*, the five happiness refer to longevity, wealth, good health, virtue, and education. These five happiness often appeared on spring couplets. Happiness is the pinnacle of all fortunes. Everything which appears in the picture is an auspicious thing, whose pronunciation in Chinese sounds like that of fortune and longevity.

◎中华五福吉祥图典

福

福 禄 寿 喜 财

万象回春

Spring comes back

《帝京景物略》："立春候，府县官吏具公服礼句芒，各以彩杖鞭牛者三，劝农业。"鞭春牛始于《周礼·月令》："出土牛以送寒气。"旧时立春前，有鞭春牛、促春耕之习。左图以赐福天官和大象表"万象"，右图为芒种神和春牛示"回春"。

It was the tradition to whip oxen to make them plough fields during the Beginning of Spring (the first solar term in Chinese). In the left picture, we can see the heavenly officer in charge of happiness and an elephant, which represents all of nature. In the right picture there is the god of grain and a spring ox, all of which means the return of spring.

万象更新

Spring comes back

　　春联："一元复始山山水水锦添花，万象更新家家户户喜临门。"图中万年青与大象，合为"万象"。万年青又为常绿吉祥植物，又有"新"意，故为"万象更新"。春节为农历一年之始，中国人对春节最为重视，祈盼新的一年"万象更新"。

　　In this picture, evergreen trees and a big elephant are combined as a metaphor for nature. Evergreen trees are not only green all year round, but also represent newness. The Chinese Spring Festival is the beginning of the lunar calendar. Therefore, the Chinese pay great attention to the Spring Festival. They hope they can have a New Year with all new things.

门神镇宅

The door god keeps houses safe

最初的门神是两个"桃人"，是神荼、郁垒的化身。继捉鬼喂虎的神荼和郁垒后，又出现了吃鬼的门神钟馗。以后则多以武将为门神，其中首推秦琼和尉迟恭。门神也有文官，以赐福天官为多。旧俗春节将门神贴在临街门上。

The earliest door god consists of two peach-shaped people. It is said that they catch ghosts and feed them to tigers. Later there appeared another door god, Zhong Kui, who eats ghosts. After Zhong Kui, people also took military officers as door gods. Sometimes, the door god can be a civil official as well. Normally they are heavenly officers in charge of blessings. It is the tradition to paste the picture of the door god on the front door facing the street during the Spring Festival.

门神守户

The door god protects
the home

驱邪迎福是古代绘画的主题思想，门神画则是中国早期绘画形式之一。战国曾侯乙墓中已有执戈立于户牗旁的神怪绘画，这应是门神的初形。《汉书》："广川惠王越，殿门有成庆画，短衣大袴长剑。"成庆是古之勇士，汉时为门神。

Chasing away evil and welcoming the spring are the main themes of old time painting. Door painting is one of the earliest types of paintings in China. There were already paintings of gods and ghosts in the Warring States Period. This was the earliest stage of the door god.

◎中华五福吉祥图典

福

福 禄 寿 喜 财

门神安舍

The door god protects the home

门神是披盔贯甲或袍带仗剑者，常贴在临街的大门上。尺幅大小不一，大者高约五尺左右，与人身高相等；小者尺余。大者多是王公官宦或豪门大户人家门上悬挂，小者多为平民百姓、柴篱板门之家于新年时贴用，以求吉祥。

The door god is normally depicted with martial attire and a sword. The size of door god paintings varies. The big ones were often hung on the walls of the houses of government officials or noble families; while the ordinary people often had smaller ones. When they are used during the Chinese New Year, they represent a blessing.

◎中华五福吉祥图典

福

福 禄 寿 喜 财

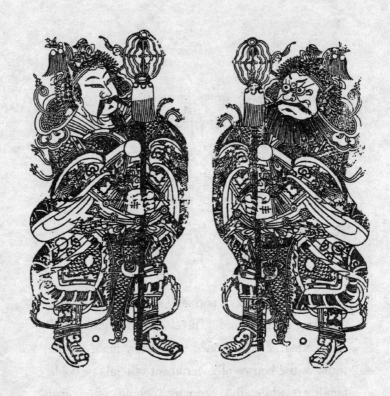

门神御鬼

*The door god keeps
ghosts away*

汉·蔡邕《独断》："海中有度朔之山，上有桃木，蟠屈三千里，卑枝东北有鬼门，万鬼所出入也。神荼与郁垒二神居其门，主阅领诸鬼，其恶害之鬼，执以苇索，食虎。故十二月岁竟，乃画荼、垒于门户，以御凶也。"

It is said that there is a mountain in the ocean, where peach woods grow for three thousand miles, and that millions of ghosts live in its northeast area. Two door gods, Shen Tu and Yu Lei, are in charge of all ghosts and feed evil ghosts to tigers. People will draw the picture of these two door gods on their doors at the end of Chinese lunar year for protection.

◎中华五福吉祥图典

福

福禄寿喜财

女娲补天

The goddess patching
the sky

女娲，是我国古代神话中创造人类的女神。相传天地开裂后，是女娲抟黄土做人，才有了人类。后水神共工与火神祝融相斗，破坏了人类的安宁生活，引起天塌地裂。于是女娲炼五色石补天，斩鳌足撑天地，拯救了人类。

Nü Wa is the goddess which created mankind in Chinese mythologies. She used mud to create human beings. Legend has it that the fight between the god of water and the god of fire destroyed the peaceful life of the world and made a big hole in the sky. It was Nü Wa who refined colored stone to fix the hole so that mankind was saved.

中华五福吉祥图典

福

福 禄 寿 喜 财

天下太平

The peaceful world

四大天王俗称四大金刚，是佛教中的神将。南方增长天王，手执宝剑，司风；东方持国天王，手执琵琶，司调；北方多闻天王，手持宝伞，司雨；西方广目天王，手中缠绕一龙，司顺。四件法宝寓意为：风调雨顺，天下太平。

The four heavenly kings are also called the Four Devas, warrior attendants in Buddhism. The southern Zengzhang King, with a sword in his hands, takes charge of wind; the eastern Chiguo King, carrying a *pipa* (a Chinese traditional musical instrument), presides over music; the northern Duowen King, taking an umbrella, governs rain; and the western Guangmu King has a dragon in his hands, keeping everything in order. These four precious Buddhist instruments imply smooth wind and rain, and a safe and harmonious world.

中华五福吉祥图典

福

福 禄 寿 喜 财

天 下 太 平

The peaceful world

《礼记·中庸》："国家将兴，必有祯祥。"国泰才能民安，所以"天下太平"是最大的吉祥。在旧时的钱币、瓦当等器物上常有"天下太平"四字。图中的 12 生肖表示年年太平，享受太平自然是大福，故图中有一"福"字。

Only when the country is stable can the ordinary people settle down. Therefore a peaceful world is the most fortunate thing on earth. These four Chinese characters can often be seen in ancient monetary currency and utensils. In the picture the twelve symbolic animals also mean that every year is a safe year. There is a big happiness character in the picture, because enjoying happiness is the most precious thing.

中华五福吉祥图典

福

福 禄 寿 喜 财

天下文明

天下文明

The civilized world

《宋书·符瑞志》："其鸣，雄曰节节，雌曰足足。晨鸣曰发明。昼鸣曰上朔，夕鸣曰归昌，昏鸣曰固常，夜鸣曰保长。"《左传》："吉，是谓凤凰于飞，和鸣锵锵。"凤凰鸣，其声锵锵悦耳，天下能闻，寓意"天下文明"。

The sound of the phoenix is very powerful and pleasant, and can be heard all over the world. This saying also implies the civilized world.

天师避邪

Heavenly master kills evils

旧时民间有请张天师驱邪捉鬼之俗，把张天师的画像或图符贴于门中，以求平安之福。在古代，每逢旧历五月初五端午节，人们用泥土捏成张天师像，以艾为头，以蒜为拳，挂在门户上避邪，此端午门饰称之为"天师艾"。

It was a tradition to ask Heavenly Master Zhang to kill evils and demons. People put his picture or symbol on their door for blessings of safety. In ancient times, during Dragon Boat Festival, people made sculptures of Heavenly Master Zhang out of clay, with his head being made of moxa and fist of garlic.

福

福 禄 寿 喜 财

天师镇宅

Heavenly Master

exorcises evil spirits

张天师在民间是镇宅守户之神。
张天师身着八卦道袍，一手执剑，一
手执净水杯，骑着老虎，以威镇五毒
——蝎子、蜈蚣、壁虎、毒蛇、蜘蛛
（或蟾蜍）。旧时，五毒对人类，尤其
是儿童威胁很大。天师可保佑合宅平
安。

Here, Heavenly Master Zhang wears an
Eight-Trigrams robe, with a sword in one hand,
and a cup of clean water in the other hand. He
rides on a tiger to crush the five poisonous creatures – scorpions, lizards, poisonous snakes, cen-
tipedes, and spiders（or toads）. In old times,
these five poisonous creatures posed a great threat
to mankind, especially to children. Heavenly
Master Zhang can protect the safety of the whole
family.

天官赐福

The heavenly officer
brings blessings

旧俗中有"三官",天官赐福，
地官赦罪，水官解厄。天官又称福
神、福星、福判等。天官一身朝服装
束，五绺长髯，慈眉善目。或手执如
意，或怀抱童子，也有的手托"天官
赐福"的条幅。天官雍容华贵，赐福
于民，很受欢迎。

There were three divine officials in old sayings. The heavenly officer blesses; the earth officer forgives, and the water officer safeguards. The
heavenly officer wears a royal robe, with a long
beard and a benign appearance. He either has a
ruyi in his hands, or holds children in his arms.
Sometimes he might also have a blessing couplet in
his hand. He looks grand and noble. He is very
popular among ordinary people as he brings blessings to all.

中华五福吉祥图典

福

福禄寿喜财

天官赐福

The heavenly officer brings blessings

此图又称之为"五子天官"。《宋史》窦仪传：仪弟俨、侃、偁、僖皆相继登科。冯道与禹钧有旧，赠诗有："灵椿一株老，丹桂五枝芳"之句。时号窦氏五龙。画中天官围绕五子，取义窦禹钧教五子皆中举登科之意。

This picture is also called five sons all become heavenly officers, because it was said that five brothers in the Tou family all passed imperial exams to become royal scholars. In this picture, his five sons surround the heavenly officer. This picture implies that Tou Yujun successfully taught his five sons to pass the imperial examination.

◎中华五福吉祥图典

福

福 禄 寿 喜 财

福

Good Fortune

天官賜福

*The heavenly officer
brings blessings*

此图为清代朱仙镇的彩色套印门神。传说"上元"是天官赐福的时辰，而春节，正是"上元"之期，故每逢春节期间，民间多贴"天官赐福"的门画，而商家则贴天官于中堂。"天官赐福"是福，双"天官赐福"则是大福。

This is a picture of colored printing of door god in Zhuxian Town in the Qing Dynasty. It was said that the Spring Festival period is the season of blessings. Therefore, people like to put the heavenly officer blessing picture on the door, while the merchants put such pictures in their stores.

◎中华五福吉祥图典

福

福 禄 寿 喜 财

福

Good Fortune

天官赐福

The heavenly officer

brings blessings

《梁元帝旨要》："上元为天官赐福之辰，中元为地官赦罪之辰，下元为水官解厄之辰。"元、明杂剧中有"天官赐福"一出，又名"大赐福"。多在喜庆或岁首之日演出。头戴天官帽，身穿玉带朝服的天官，赐的是"带子上朝"之福。

During the Yuan and Ming dynasties a heavenly god blessing play was often performed in celebration of the beginning of the New Year. In the picture the heavenly god wearing official hat and robe brings the blessing of taking sons to go to the palace.

◎中华五福吉祥图典

福

福 禄 寿 喜 财

天禄闢邪

天禄避邪

The heavenly deer
avoids evil

天鹿，是古代的一种吉祥神兽。它状异形奇，鹿形马尾，头有灵角，身有羽翼，神武无比。旧时，多饰立于阁门旁、陵墓前，以镇恶驱邪。鹿是长寿吉祥之物，天鹿更是神通广大。另古代"鹿"与"禄"音通，故还有吉祥富贵之意。

The divine deer was an auspicious animal in ancient times. It has a strange look, with a deer's body, horse's tail, and even horns and wings. The divine deer is normally placed on both sides of the door or in front of the tomb. The deer represents long life, and has a lot of magic power. Plus, its pronunciation is like that of the word "fortune". So, it also has the meaning of the wealth.

◎中华五福吉祥图典

福

福 禄 寿 喜 财

Good Fortune

太平世界

The peaceful world

086

六朵莲花中各有一符图：太极图、冏形图、两束丝图、双钱图、定胜图、对角觥图。这是一组古代流行的象征吉祥的图案，其寓意分别为天地阴阳、五湖四海、光明正大、五谷丰登、六畜兴旺、国富民强。六朵莲花寓意"六合太平"。

In each of the six lotuses there is an auspicious picture popular in old times, meaning respectively heaven and earth, Yin and Yang, honesty, harvest, wealth, safe country and strong people. Six lotuses mean peace in the world.

中华五福吉祥图典

福

福 禄 寿 喜 财

太平有象

The peaceful world

《象耕鸟耘辨》："兽之形魁者无出于象，行必端，履必深。"象的这些特点与太平盛世相和谐。象为瑞兽，寓意好的景象。象背上的宝瓶，为观音的净水瓶，亦称观音瓶，内盛圣水，滴洒能得祥瑞。"瓶"谐音"平"，寓意天下太平。

This picture features an elephant, which is harmonious with a peaceful world. The elephant is believed to be an animal which can bring good luck. The magic bottle on the elephant's back is the pure-water bottle of the Goddess of Mercy, whose water can bring good luck. Bottle also sounds like "safety" in its pronunciation. This means the peaceful world.

◎中华五福吉祥图典

福

福 禄 寿 喜 财

五客图

*The picture of
five birds*

《白虎通·田猎》："禽者何？鸟兽之总名。"《尔雅·释鸟》："二足而羽谓之禽，四足而毛谓之兽。"北宋文学家称五种瑞禽为"五客"：白鹇为间客，白鹭为雪客，白鹤为仙客，孔雀为南客，鹦鹉为西客。五客云集被视为吉兆也。

Writers in the Song Dynasty referred to the five birds as the five guests; these birds are the white magtail, the white heron, the white crane, the peacock, and the parrot. The gathering of these five birds presents a propitious scene.

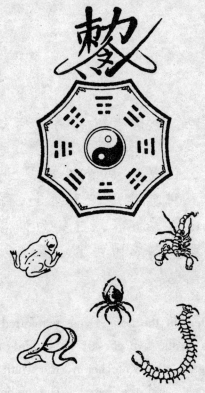

五 毒 符

The pictures of five poisonous insects

符箓，是道士用来"驱鬼招神"或"治病延年"的秘密文书。在"五毒符"的五种危害人的毒虫之上，有道家的阴阳八卦，以及"勅令"二字，表示以道家的威力可以驱五毒。旧时新年祈福或出行，禳灾之家买去焚化以求吉祥。

This is a secret Taoist symbol meaning exorcising the evil spirits and welcome the god and cure the illness and live a long life. Taoists use Eight Trigrams to show the power of Taoism, which can kill five poisonous insects. In old times, family which had suffered from ill fortune would buy these secret paper symbol and burn them at the beginning of the New Year to bring peace and luck.

◎中华五福吉祥图典

福

福 禄 寿 喜 财

五毒协合

Killing five

poisonous insects

旧时，一般称危害人类安全的蝎、蛇、蜈蚣、壁虎、蟾蜍五种虫为五毒。在我国民间的端午节时，正值五毒活跃，为避免五毒侵害儿童身体，做成五毒符给儿童佩带，以驱邪避魔，祈求安泰协合。图将五毒置于葫芦之中，求平安。

It's said that during the Chinese Dragon Boat Festival, the five poisonous insects are very active. In order to prevent children from being hurt, parents always have their children carry secret paper symbol with them. In this picture, five poisonous insects are placed inside the gourd, which implies a prayer for safety.

◎中华五福吉祥图典

福

福 禄 寿 喜 财

五福和合

The combination of

five happiness

《尚书》："五福：一曰寿，二曰富，三曰康宁，四曰攸好德，五曰考终命。"图中盒合谐音"和合"，指和合二圣。二圣蓬头笑面，一持荷花，一捧合盒，是掌管婚姻的喜神，和合之像多用于婚礼或常年悬挂中堂，取谐和之意。

In this picture, the words for "box" and "lotus" sound like "He" in Chinese, which is the name of two gods in Chinese pronunciation. These two gods are in charge of marriage. They carry a lotus and a box in their hands, with loose hair and smiling faces. This picture is often presented at weddings, or hangs all year round in conspicuous places of the house as a symbol of harmony.

◎中华五福吉祥图典

福

福禄寿喜财

日月合璧

*The sun and the moon
shine together*

《汉书·律历志上》："日月如合璧，五星如连珠。"日月同升，出现于阴历的朔日，在我国很少见。古人附会为国家的祥瑞。《诗经·小雅·天保》："如月之恒，如日之升。"日月是永恒的，江河炳地，日月恒天。

It is very rare to see the sun and the moon rising at the same time. Ancient people considered that to be a lucky sign for the nation. The sun and the moon are considered to be eternal, and so are the rivers and oceans.

日月光辉

*The sun and the moon
glory together*

唐·元稹《苦雨》："东西生日月，昼夜如转珠。"传说中周公为日神，桃花女为月神，夫妻合璧、日月同辉。在远古时期，人们就开始了对日神、月神的崇拜。日、月合而为明，日月给人带来吉光，武则天曾自创"曌"字为名。

It was said that Duke Zhou was the god of the sun, and Peach Girl was the goddess of the moon. They are husband and wife. This couple together represents the glory of the sun and the moon. The worship of the god of the sun and the goddess of the moon started in ancient times. The Chinese characters of sun and moon are combined together to create the word Ming, which means brightness. The sun and the moon together bring lucky light to people.

福

Good Fortune

取像鳥跡 始作文字
辨治万官 領理萬事

倉頡

仓颉造字

Cang Jie invented
Chinese characters

102

仓颉是传说中黄帝的史官，长着
四只眼睛，神光四射，生而能书，发
明了文字。文字，是人类文明史上最
重要的发明。仓颉庙中有联："明四
目，别六书，万世文字之祖；运一
心，赞两仪，千古士儒之师。"汉字
已有数千年的历史。

Cang Jie was the historian official of the Yellow Emperor in legend. He had four eyes. He
could read when he was born. He is said to have
invented Chinese characters, which was the most
important invention in the history of Chinese civilization. The history of Chinese characters can be
traced back to several thousand years ago.

凤羽祥云

Phoenix feather and lucky clouds

凤凰是象征和平与幸福的瑞鸟，中国古代神话中，凡祥云瑞气，有凤来仪，必有富贵吉祥。古人可凭云色观察吉凶，五彩缤纷者为祥云，黑云翻滚者为恶云。祥云是吉祥的图案，且有飘飘欲仙的意境。"凤羽祥云"是吉祥之兆。

The phoenix is an auspicious bird that symbolizes peace and happiness. In Chinese ancient mythology, colorful clouds and the appearance of a phoenix were certain to bring wealth and luck. Ancient people could read good and bad omens in the color of the clouds. The colorful cloud is a lucky sign; the black cloud is the bad one. The lucky cloud creates an atmosphere of divine heaven.

◎中华五福吉祥图典

福

福 禄 寿 喜 财

105

文运昌盛

The promising career
of civil officials

文昌崇拜，源于孔子的"学而优则仕"。文昌星意符文运昌盛，故被视为主宰文运的星宿神而奉祀。文昌君的两个侍从为天聋、地哑，以防泄密。农历二月初三是文昌帝君诞日，明、清时官员要去文昌祠祭拜，士子们梵香祷告。

The worship of the Wen Chang Star began with the Confucian saying: Those who are excellent in study will become government officials. The Wen Chang star symbol is also worshipped by people as the god who watches over students. The god of Wen Chang has two guards, which are called Heavenly Deaf and Earthly Dumb so that they couldn't disclose information. February 3rd is believed to be the birthday of the god Wen Chang. Officials in the Ming and Qing dynasties would usually pay tribute to Wen Chang Temple during this time.

中华五福吉祥图典

福

福 禄 寿 喜 财

双　福

Double happiness

　　福，指福气、福运、洪福等。《韩非子》："全寿富贵谓之福。"《千字文》中有"福缘善庆"表示福缘于善良喜庆。福乃吉祥之最，俗话说"福无双至"，得到"双福"那是千载难逢，真是大吉大利。图以两只蝙蝠环抱寓之。

Fu in Chinese means good luck, good fortune. In the *Thousand Words* (a famous book that was used in ancient times to teach children Chinese characters), Fu was said to originate in happy celebrations. Happiness is considered to be the best of all lucks. It was said that it was so hard to attain double happiness that it was considered a once-in-a-thousand-year occurrence. In the picture we can see two bats circling around the word. ("Bats" sound the same as "happiness" in Chinese.)

◎中华五福吉祥图典

福

福禄寿喜财

本固枝荣

*The flower and branches
all in blossom*

《尚书·洪范》曰："五福：一曰寿，二曰富，三曰康宁，四曰攸好德，五曰考终命。"在民间，福、禄、寿、喜、财也为"五福"。图中以五只蝙蝠喻之，从瓶中飞出。民族乐器"笙"谐音"升"。图为清代杨柳青的吉庆娃娃画。

In the *Book of Historical Documents*, five happiness refers to luck, position, longevity, happiness and wealth. There are five bats in the picture symbolizing the five happiness. This is a Yang Liuqing painting from the Qing Dynasty.

福

福 禄 寿 喜 财

平安双福

Double happiness and peace

旧时除夕，每户门前挂一方灯，以利行人，点缀年景。灯画内容多是戏出、历史故事、吉祥人物等。这是一幅清朝襄汾的灯画。刘海双手捧一宝瓶，飞来两只红蚨。以"瓶"谐音"平"，以"蚨"谐音"福"，故而题作"平双福"。

People always hung a square-shaped lamp in front of their gate for the convenience of passengers, and also for decoration on Chinese New Year's eve. The drawings on the lamp were normally chosen from drama, history stories, or depicted lucky people, etc. This is a lamp painting from the Xiangfen area in the Qing Dynasty. Liu Hai holds two magic bottles in his hand, while two red bats fly by. The bottle sounds like "peace", while the bat symbolizes happiness. So this picture means peace and double happiness.

平安有福

Happiness and peace

图为清代杨柳青的立宫间，宫间又叫"贡笺"、"工光"、"贡光"等名称。是以整张粉连纸印、绘而成，多贴在堂屋中，内容非常丰富。图中画蝴蝶、宝瓶及儿童作捕蝶、玩球游戏，象征人们对平安有福和对好生活的追求。

This is a Yang Liuqing painting from the Qing Dynasty, a full page drawing. It was normally placed in the middle of the room. In this picture, we see a butterfly, a bottle, and some children chasing butterflies and playing ball games. These all symbolize people's pursuit of peace, happiness and a good life.

朱雀　　　　青龙

玄武　　　　白虎

四　象

Four images

《易·系辞上》："两仪生四象。"四象是我国古代表示天空东、南、西、北四大区星象的四组动物，即东龙、南鸟、西虎、北龟蛇，春秋战国五行说流行后，四象配色，成为青龙、朱雀、白虎、玄武。四象也指四时，或水、火、木、金布于四方。

The dragon, bird, tiger and turtle were used in Chinese ancient times (recorded in *The Book of Changes*) as the symbols of east, south, west and north areas of the sky. It is called four images, which sometimes also indicate water, fire, wood and gold. During the Spring and Autumn and the Warring States periods, people added color to the four images. Thereafter, the symbols became a green dragon, red bird, white tiger, and black turtle.

四 君 子

Four gentlemen

明万历年间黄凤池辑《梅竹兰菊四谱》，陈继儒题称"四君"，以为"君子"的清高品德，后来又名"四君子"。梅，凌寒斗雪；兰，清雅幽香；竹，虚心劲节；菊，傲骨晚香。在群芳中被誉为"四君子"以梅兰竹菊象征人品的高尚。

The four gentlemen refer to plum blossoms, orchids, bamboo, and chrysanthemums. Plum blossoms resist snow and bloom in cold winter; orchids are elegant and fragrant; bamboo, modest and unyielding; and the chrysanthemum is proud and blooms in late autumn. They are given the title "gentlemen flowers" for their virtues. Generally, these four plants are used to symbolize noble personalities.

◎中华五福吉祥图典

福

福 禄 寿 喜 财

四　瑞　图

The pictures of four mascots

《云中献图》颂画师神笔，太极升空。《海屋添筹》写三老问年，后多作祝人长寿之词。《鱼龙变化》写鲤跃龙门成龙，遂成为祝人未来会有发迹之日的颂词。《麟凤呈祥》象征禹王治世，民享太平之乐。瑞者，吉庆祥瑞也。

The picture Presenting Drawings in the Clouds eulogizes the magic power of the painter; The Sea House is often used to wish for longevity; Fish Turns into a Dragon is used to wish for prosperity in the future; The Unicorn and the Phoenix stands for the rule of Emperor Yu, and the happiness of the people at that time. These four pictures and their lucky implications are called "the pictures of four mascots".

四时平安

Peace at all times

　　图为清代杨柳青笔绘的立宫间。绘四个可爱的童子，各抱花瓶一尊，瓶内分别插着牡丹、荷花、菊花、山茶四时应景花卉。以四季花卉示四时，以"瓶"谐音平安之"平"，合为四时平安。以示平平安安、子孙健壮、全家幸福。

This picture was from Yang Liuqing in the Qing Dynasty. Four lovely kids are holding bottles with peonies, lotus flowers, chrysanthemum, and camellia in them. These four kinds of flowers stand for the four seasons. The bottle sounds the same as "peace" in Chinese. The whole picture implies safety, healthy offspring and a happy family.

中华五福吉祥图典

福

福 禄 寿 喜 财

四季平安

Peace at all times

　　《广群芳谱》称月季花：四季不断开花，称长春花。杨万里诗："只道花无十日红，此花无日不春风。"图以花瓶中插月季花，寓"四季平安"。旧时，家中桌案上多放有花瓶，一直延续至今。月季花也早成了北京的市花。

Chinese roses blossom all year round. In this picture, there is a Chinese rose in a vase, which means safety during the four seasons. In old times, people liked to put some vases on their desks for decoration. This tradition has continued to the present day. Chinese roses are now the city flower of Beijing.

◎中华五福吉祥图典

福

福禄寿喜财

四季安泰

Peace at all times

128

四扇屏上的牡丹、荷花、菊花、梅花分别代表四季，以示春安、夏泰、秋祺、冬祥之意。后面四幅吉祥画中的猫，与"耄"谐音。《盐铁论·考养》："七十曰耄。"人活七十古来稀，除有四季安泰之吉，还有富贵长寿之详。

A peony, lotus, chrysanthemum, and plum on a painted screen stand for the four seasons in a year. The cat in the following four pictures sounds like Ao in Chinese, which refers to those older than 70 years. As the old saying goes: A man seldom lives to be 70 years old. So besides wishing for safety in all seasons, it is also a prayer for longevity.

福

福 禄 寿 喜 财

Good Fortune

春 安

Peace in spring

　　春为四季之首，立春为二十四节
气之首。春回大地，万物复苏，是最
美好的季节。相传五帝之一的少昊，
其子句芒人面鸟身，司掌农业，风调
雨顺，五谷丰登。后得道成仙，奉为
春神。旧时，每逢立春都要举行祭春
神的活动。

Spring is the first of the four seasons, and
the Beginning of Spring (one of the Chinese solar
terms) is the starting point for the 24 Chinese solar
terms. It is also the best season, when all natures
come back to life. It was said that the son of Shao
Hao (one of the five emperors), who has a human
face and a bird's body and is in charge of agricul-
ture, modulates the weather so that it brings har-
vests. Later he became a god, and so is respected
as the god of spring. In ancient times, there
would be activities at the beginning of each spring
in which sacrifices were offered to the god of spring.

夏　泰

Peace in summertime

相传立夏之时，周朝天子亲率三公九卿、王公贵族等，浩浩荡荡赴南郊迎夏，祭祀南方神祇。王安石有《初夏即事》诗："石梁茅屋有弯埼，流水溅溅度西陂。晴日暖风生麦气，绿阴幽草胜花时。"至明、清时，还增加了一些新的内容。

It was said that the Emperor of the Zhou Dynasty would take all the royal family and government officials to the southern suburbs in order to welcome the coming Summer at the Beginning of Summer (one of the Chinese solar terms), and to offer sacrifices to the southern shrine of mystery. People have added some new activities to this ritual since the Ming and Qing dynasties.

福
Good Fortune

秋 祺

Peace in autumn

春华秋实，秋天是丰收的季节。立秋时，周朝天子照例要率王公大臣到西郊迎秋，祭祀西方神祇。到了汉朝，还有根据立秋的早晚，占卜秋天凉热的习俗。到了明清，还增加了秤人、尝新、吃西瓜、祭祖等一系列的民俗活动。

Spring flowers are harvested in the fall. Autumn is the season of harvest. During the Beginning of the Autumn (one of the Chinese solar terms), it was said that the Emperor of the Zhou Dynasty would take the royal family and government officials to the western suburbs to welcome the arrival of the season, and offer sacrifice to the western shrine of mystery. After the Han Dynasty, people started to predict the weather of the coming autumn season according to the starting point of the season. People began to add other activities such as weight scaling, watermelon eating and sacrifices during the Ming and Qing dynasties.

◎中华五福吉祥图典

福

福 禄 寿 喜 财

冬　祥

Peace in winter

中华五福吉祥图典

福

福 禄 寿 喜 财

　　冬到北郊，祭祀四方之神，以求春安、夏泰、秋祺、冬祥。时至立冬，一年将尽，祭祀更加虔诚、仪式也更为隆重，以求明年风调雨顺。

It was said that the Emperor of the Zhou Dynasty would take the royal family and government officials to the northern suburbs to welcome the coming winter at the Beginning of Winter（one of the Chinese solar terms）, and to offer sacrifice to the mystery shrines of four directions for their blessing for safty in all seasons. The winter sacrifice-offering ceremonies were more religious; the ceremony was grand and everybody looked forward to a blessed New Year.

四海升平

The peaceful world

◎中华五福吉祥图典

　　四海，在这里泛指天下。《孟子·梁惠王上》："故推恩足以保四海。"升平，指太平。《汉书·梅福传》："使孝武帝听用其计，升平可致。"图中海水寓"四海"，"笙"、"瓶"寓"升平"，合为"四海升平"，即天下太平之意。

The four seas represent the whole world. Shengping here means peace. The sea water, the bottle, the musical instrument in the picture all refer to the peaceful world.

福

福禄寿喜财

四海平安

The peaceful world

龙是传说中最大的灵物。佛教中的天龙八部就有龙众，专司兴云降雨。道教中也有众多龙王，如四海龙王、五方龙王、诸天龙王等。自唐朝以来，历代帝王又封龙神为王。旧时，有水之处就有龙王庙，以求风调雨顺、四海平安。

The dragon is the largest auspicious animal in Chinese legend. In Buddhism, the dragon is in charge of the wind and clouds. In Taoism, there are many dragon kings. Since the Tang Dynasty, the emperor of every kingdom recognized the god of dragons as king. In ancient times, wherever there is water there will be temples to the dragon king, where people prayed for the blessings of good weather, and a peaceful and safe world.

中华五福吉祥图典

福

福 禄 寿 喜 财

·圖馬龍·

龍馬者天地之
精其為形也馬
身而龍鱗故謂
之龍馬龍高八尺
五寸頸骼有翼
踏水不沒聖人
在位負圖出於
孟河之中焉
易經大傅之有
曰河出圖洛出
書聖人則之是
也詳見繫辭

龙马负图

Dragon-horse carries book

张衡《东京赋》："龙图授义，龟书界似。"传说伏羲在河边见一龙马负图从水中跃出，受河图之启发明八卦。洛水中爬出一只神龟，龟背纹构成一幅图即洛书，大禹受启发将天下分为九州。"河图洛书"，河图为龙图，洛书为龟书。

It was said that Fu Xi saw dragon-horse jumping out of the water, carrying a map on its back. Fu Xi was enlightened by the map and invented Eight Trigrams. There was a turtle crawling above the water, the texture of whose shell made a picture. The Emperor Yu divided the world into nine parts after he saw this picture.

中华五福吉祥图典

福

福 禄 寿 喜 财

吉庆多福

Luck, happiness

and celebration

大福字上可爱的童子，右手执
"戟"谐音"吉"，左手提"磬"谐音
"庆"，磬上有"双鱼"谐音"双余"。
右脚蹬金钱，左脚踏元宝，胸前还佩
挂长命锁。福字上还有口衔灵芝的仙
鹤。子是福、寿是福、财是福，故为
多福。

This lovely kid carries in his right hand a
halberd, the name of which sounds like the word
for "luck" in Chinese, and in his left hand is a
chime stone, which sounds the same as "celebration" in Chinese. On the chime stone is inscribed
double fish which means abundance. He is stepping on a coin and a shoe-shaped gold, and wearing a long-life necklace. There is also a crane,
with a piece of magic fungus in its mouth. With
the addition of a big "Happiness" in the back-
ground, the whole picture implies multiple happiness, as having children is happiness, longevity is
happiness, and wealth is also happiness.

◎中华五福吉祥图典

福

福禄寿喜财

福

Good Fortune

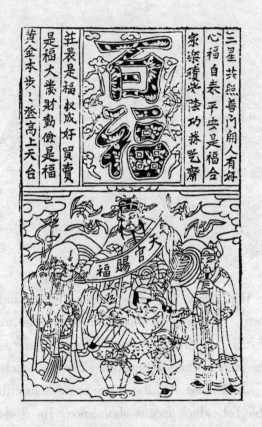

黄金本炎炎　登高上天台
是福大将财勤俭是福
庄农是福收成好买卖
宗深积庆陰功搂艺斋
心福自表平安是福合
三星共照尊门同人有好

天官賜福

百　福　图

Hundred happiness

明朝沈德符《野获编》："杂剧三星下界、天官赐福种种吉庆传奇，皆系供奉御前，呼嵩献寿，但宜教坊司、钟鼓司肄习之并勋戚贵藩鉴赏之耳。"图中的福、禄、寿三星下界，福星手中的条幅天官赐福等，似与元明杂剧有关。

In this picture we see the three gods in charge of luck, position and longevity all coming down to earth. What the god of luck holds in his hand is a couplet with the writing of "heavenly blessing", conferring luck. This may be related to dramatic works in the Yuan and Ming dynasties.

◎中华五福吉祥图典

福

福禄寿喜财

夸父追日

Kua Fu chases the sun

《山海经》："夸父与日逐走，入日。渴得饮，饮于河渭，河渭不足，北饮大泽。未至，道渴而死。弃其杖，化为邓林。"夸父是古代传说中的博父。表现出古代人类战胜自然的信念，夸父渴死时还将手杖化为邓林，以荫后人。

Kua Fu is a hero in Chinese legend, who died of thirst when chasing the sun. But he displayed a strong belief that humans can conquer nature. Before he died, he turned his stick into the forest to provide shade for his offspring.

中华五福吉祥图典

福

福 禄 寿 喜 财

全 家 福

The picture of the whole family

《周易·家人》："正家，而天下定矣。"汉·荀悦《申鉴·政体》："天下之本在家。"福、禄、寿、喜等九位神尊聚济一堂，示神之全家福。旧时节令，民间此类画贴在家中，自然是于家全福了。近代也称全家合影为"全家福"。

In ancient books, people believed that as long as they had a stable family they would have a peaceful world. When all nine gods in charge of luck, position, longevity, and happiness gather together, it represents the happy family of the gods. In old time, people liked to place this kind of picture at home for good luck. Nowadays, the picture of the whole family is also called "good fortune for the whole family".

中华五福吉祥图典

福

福禄寿喜财

伏羲画卦

*Fu Xi paints
Eight Trigrams*

《易经》："古者包牺氏之王天下也，仰则观象于天，俯则观法于地，观鸟兽之文，与地之宜，近取诸身，远取诸物，于是始作八卦，以通神明之德，以类万物之情。"伏羲被尊为人文初祖。八卦为人类最早的文字符号体系。

It's recorded in *The Book of Changes* that Eight Trigrams was invented by our ancestor to symbolize all natural phenomena. It is a link between humans and spirits.

Fu Xi is believed to be an ancestor of the Chinese people. Eight Trigrams are believed to be the earliest word or symbol system of mankind.

中华五福吉祥图典

福

福禄寿喜财

阳光普照

The sun shines

宋·赵匡胤《咏初日》："太阳初出光赫赫，千山万山如火发。一轮顷刻上天衢，逐退群星与残月。"旧俗农历二月初一为中和节，祭太阳神。《天咫偶闻》："二月初一，太阳宫进香，人家以米糕祀日，糕上以彩面作鸡形。"

February 1st in the lunar calendar is a festival for offering sacrifices to the god of the sun. People will visit the temple of the sun and pay their respects, and put chicken-shaped cookies in the sacrificial vessel.

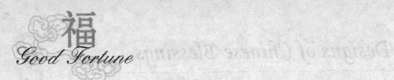

福
Good Fortune

雞王鎮宅

鸡王镇宅

*The cock safeguards
the family*

图为清代江南农村新年的门画，此习俗由来已久。梁·宗懔《荆楚岁时记》："正月一日，贴画鸡户上，悬苇索于其上，插桃符其傍，百鬼畏之。"金距花冠，翠翎锦羽的大公鸡，口啄毒虫，爪踏珍宝，气宇轩昂地立门镇宅。

This is the door painting used during the New Year in the southern part of the Yangtze river region during the Qing Dynasty. People paste the picture of a rooster in front of the door, high above, with the intention of scaring away evil spirits, because the cock will eat all poisonous insects. The cock in the painting, with a poisonous insect in its mouth, treads proudly on the treasures and protects the family. This tradition has been observed for a long time.

中华五福吉祥图典

福

福 禄 寿 喜 财

花好月圆

The beautiful flower
and the round moon

Designs of Chinese Blessings

旧时婚联中有："洞房花烛夜，花好月圆时。"花好月圆象征美满团聚，一般多做新婚颂词。传说中专司人间婚姻的神是月下老人，他在月下翻阅天下婚牍，袋中藏着"红线"，暗系在男女双方的脚上，使二人结为百年之好。

The theme of the beautiful flower and the round moon usually symbolizes the harmony of marriage. It is normally used for the blessing of newly-weds. It was said in legend that the god in charge of marriage is an old man, who reads all information related to the marriage of common human beings by moonlight. He uses the red thread in his pocket to link the feet of the man and the woman and make them become couple.

中华五福吉祥图典

福

福 禄 寿 喜 财

159

连 年 有 福

Continuous fortune

大福字两对角的莲花，是圣洁吉
祥之花，以"莲"谐音"连"。大福
字另两对角鲶鱼，以"鲶"谐音
"年"，以"鱼"谐音"余"，寓意
"连年有余"。连年有余自然是老百姓
的"大福"。旧时，家中多贴带有吉
祥图的福字。

The lotus on two sides of the big "luck"
character is a kind of sacred flower. There are also
two catfish on the other two sides. Catfish sounds
like "year" and "surplus" and lotus sounds "continuous", together meaning a continuing surplus.
In old times, most families liked to post the big
"luck" character with an auspicious painting.

◎中华五福吉祥图典

福

福 禄 寿 喜 财

福

Good Fortune

迎春降福

Welcome spring with a blessing

汉·乐府古辞《长歌行》："阳春布德泽，万物生光辉。"唐·钱起《春郊》："东风好作阳和使，逢草逢花报发生。"《宋史·乐志七》："阴和启蛰，品物皆春。"图以迎春花示迎春，以蝙蝠示福。"迎春降福"寓意春回大地，福满人间。

Winter jasmine is used in this picture to welcome spring, and the bat is considered a sign of good luck. The whole picture implies that luck is with people when spring comes back.

汲水泽民

Water benefits people

远古时的"五祀"是指门、户、井、灶、土五神。井和人们的生活息息相关，过去吃水主要靠井。井神属于家神，一般没有自己的庙宇，塑像也很少。少数井旁造有神龛，供奉井神，汲水泽民。有的井神有两位：水井公、水井婆。

Five sacrifices in ancient time were made to the gods of door, house, well, kitchen and earth. Wells were closely related to people's lives, as people mainly relied on wells to get water. The god of wells belongs to the god of the household. There is no particular temple or shrine for the god of wells, neither is there a specific statue. There is niche for the worship of the god, near a few wells. Sometimes the god of wells is depicted as a pair of old people.

Good Fortune

纳福迎祥

Accept happiness and welcome fortune

《庄子注疏》："吉者福善之事，祥者嘉庆之征。"福是吉祥的核心。五只蝙蝠寓意"五福"。蝙蝠作为吉祥物由来已久，主要是"蝠"与"福"同音，沾了"福"的光。图中一童子作"纳福"状，另一童子作"迎祥"状。

Luck is the core of auspiciousness. Five bats represent the five blessings. The bat has been an auspicious animal for a long time, because of its similar pronunciation to "luck". In the picture there is one child poised to accept Luck, and the other is welcoming Luck.

◎中华五福吉祥图典

福

福禄寿喜财

阿弥陀佛

Namomitabhaya

　　佛教是世界三大宗教之一，大约
已有二千五百余年的历史。佛祖释迦
牟尼，是佛教的创始人。佛，即佛
陀。是梵语的音译。意译应该是"智
者"，是至高无上的智慧。"南无阿弥
陀佛"的汉意："衷心礼拜彻察一切的
智者。"

Buddhism is one of the three most popular religions in the world, with about 2,500 years of history. Sakyamuni was the founder of Buddhism. Buddha is the sound from the Indian words, which means one with unfathomable wisdom. Namomitabhaya in Chinese means the whole-hearted worship of all those with wisdom and thorough observation.

中华五福吉祥图典

福

福 禄 寿 喜 财

画龙点睛

Painted dragon's eye

唐·张彦远《历代名画记》："武帝崇饰佛寺,多命僧繇画之……金陵安乐寺四白龙,不点睛眼。每云:'点睛即飞去。'人以为妄诞,固请点之。须臾,<u>雷电破壁</u>,两龙乘云腾去上天,二龙未点睛者见在。"常喻关键一举。

As the legend goes, an emperor in the Tang Dynasty once asked someone to paint dragons on the walls of a temple. Four dragons were painted on the wall without eyes. The man said the dragons would fly away if their eyes were added. No one believed him. So the man added eyes for two of the dragons. Suddenly the two dragons with eyes moved and flew into the clouds, while the two dragons without eyes remained there still. This term normally refers to a critical action which is required to complete something, or to set something in motion.

◎中华五福吉祥图典

福

福禄寿喜财

国色天香

Divine beauty of
the nation

牡丹，是中国传统的名花，兼有
色、香、韵三者之美，令人倾倒。
《本草纲目》："群花品中，以牡丹第
一。"唐·李正封诗云："国色朝酣酒，
天香夜染衣。"从此牡丹便有了"国
色天香"之美誉。后来，多以此称誉
妇人之雍容华贵。

The peony is a famous flower in Chinese tradition, with beauty, color and fragrance. People
are always enchanted by its beauty. Therefore, the
peony is known as the divine beauty of the nation.
Later, people used this term to describe a
woman's beauty.

河清海晏

Clear river and peaceful ocean

《拾遗记》："黄河千年一清，清则圣人生于此时。"《周诗》："俟河之清，人寿几何？"晏，意为安也。"河清海晏"寓意太平盛世，天下大治。图中以"荷"谐音"河"，"燕"谐音"晏"，又取河水之"清"，海棠之"海"，合为"河清海晏"。

In the picture, lotus is used for its sound, which is similar as that of "river", swallow is also used for its sound, like that of the word "peaceful". Likewise, in Chinese crabapple sounds like "ocean". Combined, this picture means clear and peaceful rivers and oceans, implying a peacefully ruled world.

宝 相 花

Buddha flower

　　宝相，是佛教徒对佛像的庄严称呼。宝相花，是一种象征意义上的花。随着佛教在中国的盛行，宝相花已成为中国传统吉祥纹饰的一种。它集中了莲花、牡丹花、菊花的特征，更主要是吸收了莲花的特征，成为理想的花型。

Baoxiang, meaning treasured statue, is the respectful name for Buddhist statue. This flower is actually a fictitious one. With the spread of Buddhism in China, cloth decorated with this flower pattern became one of the traditional auspicious fabrics in China. It combines the features of lotus, peony and chrysanthemum together, and mostly draws on the features of the lotus as an ideal flower.

福

Good Fortune

廟祖洲湄

平安　　祈求

妈祖保佑

The blessing of Goddess Matsu

妈祖原名林默，北宋建隆元年诞生在福建莆田的湄洲屿。水性极好，常救助人于海难，后被神化为海上保护神，被历代帝王多次册封为"天妃"等。自宋代湄洲岛建了第一座妈祖庙起，至今妈祖庙已遍布世界各地，祈求航海平安。

Goddess Matsu was born on Meizhou Island of Putian, Fujian Province in the Northern Song Dynasty. She was said to be extremely good at swimming, and she always saved those in danger at sea. Later, she was named the protecting goddess of the ocean. She was also conferred with the title of divine lady many times by different emperors. There are many Matsu temples around the world since the establishment of the first one on Meizhou Island in the Song Dynasty. People visit these temples and pray for safe trips on the ocean.

◎中华五福吉祥图典

福

福 禄 寿 喜 财

祈求平安

Praying for peace

妈祖又称天后，是海神娘娘。旧时，沿海人民为了祈求出海安全，修建了许多妈祖庙。农历三月二十三是妈祖诞辰，朝拜者人山人海，以求"风调雨顺，国泰民安"。图中千里眼、顺风耳是天后护卫神，哪吒也可镇海求安。

Goddess Matsu is also called the goddess of the ocean. Long ago, coastal people built many Matsu temples to pray for safety on the ocean. Many people go to Matsu temples on the 23rd of March (in the lunar calendar), which is said to be Matsu's birthday. They want Goddess Matsu to bring pleasant weather and safety. In this picture, there are also other guarding gods.

◎中华五福吉祥图典

福

福 禄 寿 喜 财

钟馗

钟馗贴家中挑剧
斩妖莉镇宅能
除邪合家
享太平

钟馗镇宅

Zhong Kui safeguards

the homestead

中华五福吉祥图典

福

福 禄 寿 喜 财

　　钟馗的形象多是：铁面虬髯，豹头虎眼，身着红袍，足蹬皂靴，手持利剑，脚踩小鬼。民间多贴于家中，以斩妖除邪、守户镇宅。图中有文："钟馗贴家中，执剑斩妖精。镇宅能除邪，合家享太平。"民间关于钟馗的传说很多。

Most of Zhong Kui's images are like this: a hard face, curly beard, leopard head, and tiger eyes. He wears red robes and high boots, with a sharp sword in his hands, and is stepping over a little ghost. His picture is normally placed in the home to chase away evil spirits, and bring safety. There are many stories about Zhong Kui in Chinese folklore.

福

Good Fortune

钟馗增福

Zhong Kui brings

happiness and luck

《平鬼传》：钟馗驾祥云，神荼变成一只蝙蝠在前引路，郁垒化作一把宝剑伏于馗背，众鬼紧随其后。蝙蝠之"蝠"与"福"谐音，表示幸福来临。钟馗是斩妖驱邪之神，岁初家家挂钟馗像，蝙蝠也使钟馗有了"增福"的神通。

It was said that Zhong Kui rode on auspicious clouds, with a bat leading the way in front of him, and he carried a magic sword on his back, followed by many ghosts. The word for bat sounds the same as luck and happiness in Chinese. Zhong Kui is a god who kills evil spirits. People hang Zhong Kui's picture at the beginning of Chinese New Year. The bat simply increases the magic power of Zhong Kui.

钟馗除妖

Zhong Kui kills evils

　　传说钟馗原是一名进士，考中状元，不料唐德宗以貌取人，嫌其丑陋，将他赶出宫廷。钟馗当场撞殿阶而亡，死后为鬼首。唐《切韵》："钟馗之说，盖自六朝之前，因已有之，流传执鬼，非一日矣。"也有把钟馗视为判官的。

　　It was said that Zhong Kui was a scholar and had passed the imperial examinations. Unfortunately, the emperor at that time only paid attention to one's looks. The emperor chased Zhong Kui away from the palace because of his ugly face. Zhong committed suicide there on the spot by smashing himself into a palace pillar. He became the leader of the ghosts after he died. Some people consider Zhong Kui to be the judge of the underworld.

Good Fortune

钟馗辟邪

Zhong Kui kills evils

《旧京遗事》："禁中岁除，各宫门改易春联，及安放绢画钟馗神像。像以三尺长素木小屏装之，缀铜环悬挂，最为精雅。先数日各宫颁钟馗神于诸皇亲家。"唐、宋以来，皇帝每岁暮以钟馗与历日同赐大臣，可见钟馗影响之大。

Since the Tang and Song dynasties, emperors would give calendars with Zhong Kui's picture to his entire royal family and officials at the end of every year. From this we can see the depth of Zhong Kui's influence.

中华五福吉祥图典

福

福 禄 寿 喜 财

福
Good Fortune

钟馗嫁妹

Zhong Kui plays matchmaker for his sister

钟馗进京赴考，因其像貌丑陋被
皇帝免去状元，盛怒之下，撞阶而
死。与他一同应试的同乡好友杜平将
他安葬。杜平为人好善乐施，钟馗深
感杜平恩义，遂骑驴亲率鬼卒于除夕
返回家中，亲自将妹妹嫁给杜平，以
结百年之好。

After Zhong Kui's death, his countryman and
friend Du Ping buried him. Du Ping was a very
kind and benevolent person. Zhong Kui admired
him greatly, and so married his sister to Du Ping
at Chinese New Year's Eve, in the company of a
group of ghosts.

中华五福吉祥图典

福

福 禄 寿 喜 财

神鸡驱虫

Magic cock kills insects

《风俗通》：“以雄鸡着门上，以和阴阳。”《花镜》：“雄能角胜，且能辟邪。”雄鸡作为吉祥物，辟邪是其功能之一。旧时人们在生活中对毒虫的危害很伤脑筋，除了动手灭虫外，还要借助神的力量驱虫，这也是一幅旺相符箓。

In Chinese folklore, the cock is an auspicious animal. Cocks were believed to be capable of expelling evil. In olden times people had a great deal of trouble with poisonous insects. Besides their own efforts, they also had to rely on the power of the gods. This is also a picture of good fortune.

中华五福吉祥图典

福

福 禄 寿 喜 财

Good Fortune

神虎镇宅

*Magic tiger safeguards
the homestead*

汉·应劭《风俗通义》："虎者阳物，百兽之长也。能执博挫锐，噬食鬼魅。"上古时神荼与虞缚以苇索执以食虎，于是后人常画虎于门，以辟邪驱祟。图为清代陕西凤翔瑞符，双虎张口竖尾，伏身欲博状，镇宅保四季平安。

It is said that the tiger is masculine in nature, and it is thought to be the king of all animals. In ancient times, Shen Tu and Yu Fu were said to feed tigers with ghosts. Later people painted tigers on their doors to chase away evil. This picture was originally from Fengxiang, Shaanxi Province in the Qing Dynasty. In the picture two tigers open their mouths and erect their tails, ready to fight for the safety of the family.

中华五福吉祥图典

福

福 禄 寿 喜 财

神鹰镇宅

Magic eagle safeguards
the homestead

"三节鹰"形式流行山东，因它画面有三节人物故事，下有一神鹰抓狐精而得名，每幅两条，呈对称形式，尺寸小者称"小条鹰"。图中鹰抓人物源于小说《封神演义》，有黄飞虎以神鹰抓伤妲己的故事。有神鹰镇宅，自能驱妖除灾。

This drawing is popular in Shandong Province. Its name originated in the content of the drawing, which tells three stories, with an eagle catching an embodied fox under the description. It is symmetrical. Each couplet has two pictures. Its content comes from the story of the divine eagle scratching Da Ji (a famous beauty in history). With the eagle in the house, it is believed that people will not be bothered by ghosts anymore.

中华五福吉祥图典

福

福 禄 寿 喜 财

菩萨保佑

*The blessing of
the Bodhisattvas*

菩萨是菩提菩埵的音译，唐僧法
藏释："菩提，此谓之'觉'；萨埵，
此曰'众生'。以智上求菩提，用悲
下救众生。"在佛教中菩萨仅位次于
佛，帮助佛普度众生。中国的四大菩
萨：观音、文殊、普贤、地藏。菩萨
保佑，一切平安。

This is from a translation of Indian Buddhist
scripture. In Buddhism, Bodhisattvas are in the
second place below Buddha, and their purpose is
to help deliver all mortals from torment. Four Bodhisattvas inChina are the Goddess of Mercy, Manjusri, Samantabhadra and the God of Earth. It is
said that with the blessing of Bodhisattvas, everything will be safe.

中华五福吉祥图典

福

福 禄 寿 喜 财

救苦救難菩薩

观音菩萨

The Goddess of Mercy

观世音，唐时因避太宗李世民名讳，略其"世"称"观音"至今。《注维摩诘经》："世有危难，称名自归，菩萨欢其音声，即得解腹也。"观音最早为男身像，唐以后渐成女身像。观音表"大悲"，道场在普陀山，观音在中国最受敬拜。

The Goddess of Mercy's original name is Guang Shi Yin. Because the emperor's name contains the character shi, no one else was allowed to use that character. The Goddess of Mercy originally had a man's body, but became female after the Tang Dynasty. The Goddess of Mercy means lots of suffering. Its ritual location is in Putuo Mountain. The Goddess of Mercy is widely worshipped in China.

中华五福吉祥图典

福

福禄寿喜财

文殊菩萨

Manjusri

文殊，全称文殊师利，是梵文音译，意为妙吉祥。文殊表"大智"，道场在五台山。大乘经典多因文殊发问而说。文殊是佛祖的左胁侍，顶结五髻，表示大日如来之五智；手持利剑，表示智慧锐利；坐骑青狮，表示为佛法之师。

Manjusri represents supreme wisdom. He performed Buddhist rites in Mt. Wutai. Manjusri is the bodyguard on the left side of Sakyamuni, with winded hair and carrying sharp sword, which implies brilliant wisdom. He rides on a green lion, which implies that he is a master of Buddhism.

普贤菩萨

Samantabhadra

普贤是佛祖的右胁侍，表"大行"，道场在峨嵋山。普贤是遍一切处；贤，是最妙善义。普贤坐骑六牙白象，六牙表六度，四足示四如意，白为无尘无染，象有大力为法力巨大。普贤把佛门的"善"，普及到处，功德无量。

Samantabhadra, representing kindness, is the bodyguard on the right side of Sakyamuni. He performed Buddhist rites in Mt. Emei. Samantabhadra rides a white elephant with six teeth. The elephant is pure and powerful. Samantabhadra is said to spread the kindness of Buddhism everywhere.

地藏菩萨

The God of Earth

地藏表"大愿",道场在九华山。
《地藏菩萨本愿经》载:地藏因救度
死后堕地狱的母亲而发大愿:"众生
度尽,方证菩提,地狱不空,誓不成
佛。"地藏受释迦牟尼嘱托于佛灭迹
后,弥勒佛未生前,度化娑婆世界受
苦受难的众生。

The name of the God of Earth means big
wishes. The god's ritual location is in Mt. Ji-
uhua. After Sakyamuni passed away, and before
the birth of Maitreya, the God of Earth was asked
by Sakyamuni to help all the suffering people to be
relieved.

◎中华五福吉祥图典

福

福禄寿喜财

常羲浴月

Chang Xi bathes
in the moonlight

《山海经·大荒西经》载："有女子方浴月。帝俊妻常羲，生月十有二，此始浴之。"有书称帝俊即帝舜，其妻生月十二个，生日十个，始有日月。日升东海，昼行，落入西海；月升西海，夜行，落入东海。故有浴月、浴日之说。

There once was a woman named Fang Yuyue, who gave birth to ten suns and twelve moons. After that, there was a sun and moon in the world. The sun was believed to rise from the East Ocean, and move during the daytime into the West Ocean, while the moon rises from the West ocean, and moves at night into the East Ocean.

鹿鶴同春

The deer and crane
together celebrate spring

《庄子·齐物论》："六合之外，圣人存而不论。"《疏》："六合，天地四方。"亦泛指天下。图以"鹿"谐音"六"，"鹤"谐音"合"，"桐"谐音"同"，另花开在"春"，合为"六合同春"。春者四季之始，生机盎然。寓意天下太平，欣欣向荣。

The deer in the picture has the same pronunciation as "six", and crane sounds like "harmony" in Chinese. This picture shows a blooming scene at the beginning of spring, which refers to the peaceful world and a promising future.

鹿鹤同春

The deer and crane
together celebrate spring

　　"鹿鹤"谐音"六合"。六合除指天地四方，还是古代历法用语。《淮南子》："六合，孟春与孟秋为合，仲春与仲秋为合……"另外，六合还是阴阳家所指吉利时辰。《南齐书》："十二辰为六合。"故"鹿鹤同春"也指四季同春。

　　Deer and crane sounds like "six harmony" in Chinese, which refers to the whole world in Chinese ancient sayings. This saying was mentioned in ancient Chinese calendric system. Fortune-tellers also considered it to be a fortunate date. The term means that every season is as nice as spring.

中华五福吉祥图典

福

福 禄 寿 喜 财

鹤鹿同春

*The deer and crane
together celebrate spring*

　　旧时常说："裁下梧桐树，引来金凤凰。"梧桐是美好婚姻的象征。"桐"又与"同"谐音，"同春"则表示夫妻偕老，永葆青春。鹤是长寿之征，鹿是祥瑞之兆，表示夫妻百年长寿。旧时常将"鹿鹤同春"与"鹤鹿同春"混淆。

　　The Chinese parasol is a symbol of a happy marriage; parasol of spring in Chinese sounds like "sharing spring" which means that loving couples can forever keep young. The crane represents longevity, and the deer stands for luck. Together they mean longevity for couples.

◎中华五福吉祥图典

福

福禄寿喜财

翘盼福音

Looking forward to luck

《抱朴子》："千岁蝙蝠，色如白雪，集则倒悬，脑重故也。此物得而阴干末服之，令人寿万岁。"蝙蝠为长寿之物，又有"福"音。身挂长命锁的可爱童子，翘首而盼蝙蝠的到来。以喻翘盼福音。以蝙蝠为题的吉祥图不胜枚举。

The bat is an animal which symbolizes long life as well as luck, as sound for "bat" in Chinese is very close to "luck". Young children wear long-life lock and all look forward to the bat coming, in expectation of good news. There are so many bat-related pictures that we can hardly mention all of them.

中华五福吉祥图典

福

福禄寿喜财

217

逼鼠蚕猫

A cat scaring a rat away
from eating the silkworms

Designs of Chinese Blessings

　　“逼鼠蚕猫”是江浙一带蚕农贴于家门的画。传说老鼠吃蚕，贴此门画可提醒人们防止鼠害。另一方面，蚕很娇嫩，怕冷、怕脏、怕异味，串门闲人望此门画，便知此家正在养蚕，便可自觉“闲人止步”。图为清代桃花坞彩印。

　　This picture was popular in the silkworm farmers' houses near the lower Yangtze river area. It was said that rats ate silkworms. This picture is used to warn people to keep the rats away. On the other hand, silkworms are of fragile nature and can't bear coldness, dirt or bad odors. This picture can also be used to remind visitors that the family is raising silkworms, so that they should stop at the door. This picture was printed in color in the Qing Dynasty.

中华五福吉祥图典

福

福禄寿喜财

紫气东来

The appearance of
the purple cloud

Designs of Chinese Blessings

传说函谷关令尹见有紫气从东而来，知将有圣人过关，果然老子骑青牛前来，便请老子在馆驿住下来写了《道德经》。后人则以"紫气东来"表示祥瑞。在颐和园谐趣园附近的一座门楼上，分别题有"赤城霞起"和"紫气东来"之句。

Legend has it that one day a magistrate saw purple clouds coming from the east, he thought a sage was coming soon. Just as expected, Laozi came along riding a black ox. The magistrate invited Laozi to settle down at a posthouse where Laozi wrote *The Classic of the Virtue of the Tao*. Later "purple clouds from the east" is regarded as a sign of good luck. You can also see this term in the Summer Palace in Beijing.

中华五福吉祥图典

福

福 禄 寿 喜 财

Good Fortune

紫微高照

The shining of the Zi Wei star

紫微星在古代星相崇拜中占有重
要地位，由于天官住在紫微上官，紫
微星君便成了赐福天官，紫微高照则
是吉祥赐福的象征。紫微星君曾受大
禹之命擒住水神无支祈，以铁索锁住
压在淮水之龟山脚下，从此水灾减
轻。

Zi Wei is a very important star in the Chinese
constellation system. Because the heavenly officers
reside in Zi Wei Palace, the star with the same
name became the blessed heavenly officer who was
asked by Emperor Yu to capture the water god,
and lessen the damage done by floods. When Zi
Wei shines above in the night sky, blessings,
good fortune and good luck all beckon.

中华五福吉祥图典

福

福禄寿喜财

紫微星君

The shining of
the Zi Wei star

上古时期，淮水水神无支祈为害，大禹派兵将前往征服，反被无支祈战败。大禹又派掌管时间之天神庚辰前往，无支祈被庚辰俘获。大禹又下令将无支祈用铁索锁住，压在淮水之龟山脚下，降住水灾。功臣庚辰即紫微星君。

Zi Wei is said to be a god who is in charge of time. He conquered the god of water in Huai River and used an iron lock to bind the water god at the foot of Turtle Mountain, thus totaly controlled the flood.

中华五福吉祥图典

福

福 禄 寿 喜 财

铺首护宅

The doorknob decoration

protects the family

铺首，是旧时宅门上衔门环的底座，多作虎、螭、龟、蛇等形。用以护宅守户，保平安。《汉书·哀帝纪》："孝元庙殿门铜龟蛇铺首鸣。"汉代寺庙多装饰铺首以避邪，源于上古人们对神兽的崇拜，后广泛用于官庭府院之门。

Doorknob decorations are usually at the base of doorknobs of old houses, and are shaped like tigers, snakes, turtles, etc. They are used to protect the family. They are normally used in temples during the Han Dynasty to keep away the evil spirits and also used as decorations because of ancient people's worship of sacred animals. Later they were widely used for the gates of palaces.

◎中华五福吉祥图典

福

福禄寿喜财

福　运

Fortune

蝙蝠，因其首及身如鼠，亦有
"飞鼠"、"仙鼠"之称。《抱朴子》：
"千岁蝙蝠，色如白雪，集则倒悬，
脑重故也。此物得而阴干末服之，令
人寿万岁。"蝙蝠为长寿之物，又与
"福"谐音，故在吉祥图中常有。五
只蝙蝠与祥云，寓"福运"。

Because its head and body are similar to that
of a rat, the bat is referred to as a flying rat, or
spirit rat. The bat represents long life, and sounds
like "luck" in Chinese. It is often seen in auspicious paintings. Five bats and clouds together imply good fortune.

福 到 了

Fortune arrives

《宣和画谱》："五代时人陆晃有
'天曹赐福真君'象一帧，然则今所
称天官赐福者，亦有本矣。"至宋元
民间遂以天官为福神，与禄、寿并
列，图中以"倒"寓"到"，天官赐
福，自然是福"到"了。天官五绺长
髯、慈眉善目。

Since the Song Dynasty, people have put the
heavenly officers in charge of fortune, position and
longevity together. In Chinese, "upside down"
has the same pronunciation as "arrival". The
heavenly officer in the picture has long beard and
a benign countenance.

福从天降

Fortune arrives from heaven

福者幸福也，旧谓福气、福分，与祸相对。《老子》："福兮祸之所伏，祸兮福之所隐。"《韩非子》卷六："全寿富贵之谓福。"在传统吉祥图中，蝙蝠表示"福"。"福从天降"是老天的赐予，正是：人逢吉祥日，福从天降时。

Happiness is the opposite of disaster. But according to Laozi, in good fortune lurks calamity and in calamity lies good fortune. In traditional auspicious paintings, the bat means happiness because of the similarity in pronunciation. The arrival of happiness fromheaven is seen as a blessing from the god.

中华五福吉祥图典

福

福 禄 寿 喜 财

福在眼前

Fortune in front of your eyes

每逢春节，北京白云观有"打金钱眼"的活动，以祈新年发财。古代钱币，多为方孔圆形，文称"孔方兄"。其方孔又称"钱眼"，在图中寓意"眼前"。作为吉祥物的蝙蝠，其在吉祥图中的重要作用皆因"蝠"与"福"谐音。

Every Spring Festival, there are games of shooting the square hole in the coin at White Cloud Temple, in order to wish for good luck in the New Year. Ancient coins were round in shape with square holes in the center. These holes were called the eyes of the money, here implying "in front of your eyes".

Together with the bats, the picture conveys the message of "fortune just in front of you."

中华五福吉祥图典

福

福 禄 寿 喜 财

福星高照

*The shining of
the lucky star*

福神，源于古代星相崇拜中的福星，即木星。道教把三官（天官、地官、水官）中的天官，作为福神信奉，即"天官赐福"。传说汉武帝时刺史杨成，因抵制给皇帝进贡侏儒，救百姓于水火之中，被敬奉为降福解厄的"福神"。

The god of luck was originated in the ancient worship of Jupiter. In Taoism, people named the heavenly officer as the god of luck, and prayed to him for blessings. It's said during the Han Dynasty, an official named Yang Cheng refused to pay tributes with dwarfs and saved the people from misery. People regarded him as a god of luck.

福缘善庆

Celebrate happiness

and fortune

空中飞翔的一只蝙蝠，"蝠"与"福"谐音。老者右手柱杖，杖上挂有香橼，又名枸橼，"橼"与"缘"谐音。老者左手持扇，"扇"与"善"谐音。老者身背提磬的童子，另一童子作击磬状，"磬"与"庆"谐音。合为"福缘善庆"之意。

In this drawing, the old man has in his left hand a fan, which sounds similar to "kindness" and citron hangs on the stick in his right hand implying luck. He also carries a child on his back, who is playing a chime stone which has the same pronunciation as "celebration". This picture implies luck, benevolence and celebration.

福
Good Fortune

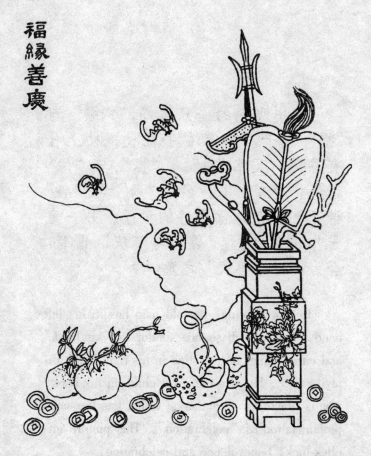

福緣善慶

福缘善庆

*Celebrate happiness
and fortune*

"福缘善庆"这一吉祥词语，源自南朝的《千字文》。《韩非子》："全寿富贵之谓福。"如果人生在世能与"福"有缘，则是最大的幸福。但如何才与福有缘，清代《训蒙增广改本》有句："人有善念，天必从之。""善人福大"。

This term came from the Southern Dynasty's famous book *Thousand Words*. The greatest happiness would be if one could be lucky all his or her life. But in order to have great luck all the time, one should be kind, as is mentioned in a piece of work of the Qing Dynasty.

鹦鹉濡羽

The parrot saves

animals from the fire

　　传说一只鹦鹉看到一山中起火，因曾受到此山鸟兽的善待，即入水濡羽，飞而洒之，以救山火。天神说你这点水怎能救火，鹦鹉说我曾侨居此山，不忍看到鸟兽遭难。于是山神受感灭火。寓意人生要重情义，朋友有难，濡羽相助。

This saying originated in folklore. It was said a mountain once caught on fire, and a parrot who had been treated kindly by animals living on the mountain tried its best to put out the fire by dipping its wings in water and carrying drops of water to the fire. God was touched and helped to put out the fire. This saying means that one should help one's friend when they are in need, even though one's capability is very limited.

◎中华五福吉祥图典

福

福 禄 寿 喜 财

夔龙拱璧

The leader of the
dragon group and jade